The Human Body

by Connie Jankowski

Science Contributor
Sally Ride Science
Science Consultants
Thomas R. Ciccone, Science Educator
Ronald Edwards, Science Educator

MISSION: SCIENCE

Developed with contributions from Sally Ride Science™

Sally Ride
Science

Sally Ride Science™ is an innovative content company dedicated to fueling young people's interests in science.

Our publications and programs provide opportunities for students and teachers to explore the captivating world of science—from astrobiology to zoology.

We bring science to life and show young people that science is creative, collaborative, fascinating, and fun.

To learn more, visit www.SallyRideScience.com

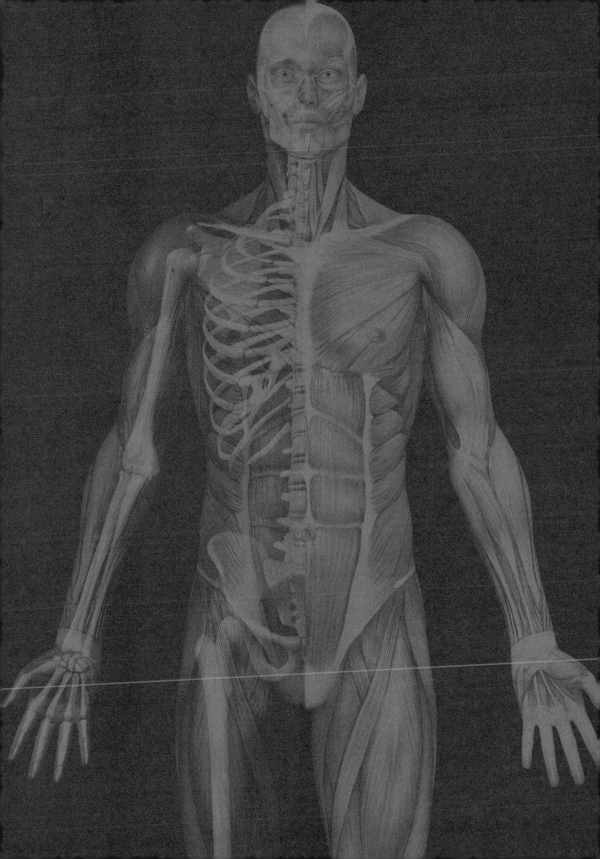

First hardcover edition published in 2009 by
Compass Point Books
1710 Roe Crest Drive
North Mankato, MN 56003

Editor: Mari Bolte
Designer: Heidi Thompson
Editorial Contributor: Sue Vander Hook

Art Director: LuAnn Ascheman-Adams
Creative Director: Joe Ewest
Editorial Director: Nick Healy
Managing Editor: Catherine Neitge

 This book was manufactured with paper containing at least 10 percent post-consumer waste.

Library of Congress Cataloging-in-Publication Data
Jankowski, Connie.
  The human body / by Connie Jankowski.
     p. cm. — (Mission: Science)
  Includes index.
  ISBN 978-0-7565-4230-6 (library binding)
  1. Body, Human—Juvenile literature. 2. Human physiology—Juvenile
literature. I. Title. II. Series.
  QP37.J36 2009
  612—dc22   2009002817

Visit Compass Point Books on the Internet at *www.capstonepub.com*
or e-mail your request to *custserv@compasspointbooks.com*

Table of Contents

The Amazing Human Body

More than 6.7 billion humans live on Earth. Each person acts and thinks differently and has a unique appearance.

However, humans share the same basic physical structure—a head, neck, torso, two arms, and two legs. The body is made up of 206 bones, 600 muscles, and 22 internal organs, which work together to keep the body alive and functioning.

Did You Know?

Humans are born with 350 bones. As the body grows, some bones fuse together, reducing the total number of bones to 206.

There are 12 major systems that make up the complex human machine:

- Cardiovascular
- Respiratory
- Digestive
- Urinary
- Endocrine
- Immune
- Reproductive
- Lymphatic
- Integumentary
- Skeletal
- Muscular
- Nervous

Ancient Medicine

Long ago, people believed that many diseases were punishments from the gods or curses cast by evil spirits. One procedure, known as bloodletting, involved cutting a vein. This was commonly used until the late 19th century. It was believed it would help cure disease.

Ancient Egyptians were one of the first people to use herbs and drugs to treat medical problems. They also performed some surgeries. However, anesthesia was unknown at that time. One way to knock out a patient was to hit him on the head with a mallet!

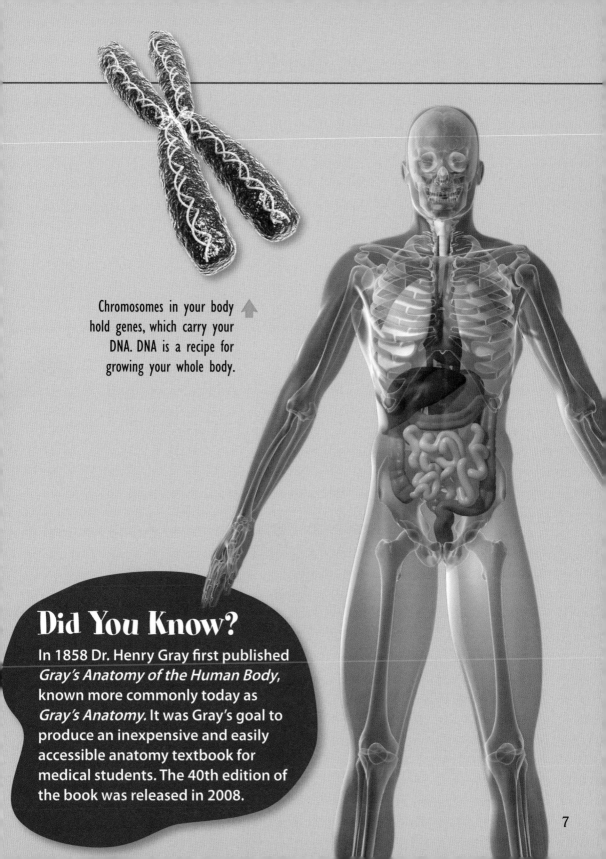

Chromosomes in your body hold genes, which carry your DNA. DNA is a recipe for growing your whole body.

Did You Know?

In 1858 Dr. Henry Gray first published *Gray's Anatomy of the Human Body,* known more commonly today as *Gray's Anatomy.* It was Gray's goal to produce an inexpensive and easily accessible anatomy textbook for medical students. The 40th edition of the book was released in 2008.

The Human Body System

The human body is an amazing machine. Many parts work together in unison to allow the body to function correctly.

The human body is constantly active. It allows people to perform daily activities that are often taken for granted, such as walking, lifting, and even breathing. Each system depends on the other systems to function. No system works independently of the others. If something goes wrong with one system, other systems, or even the entire body, may not work properly. Understanding how the body works will help us make choices that will keep our bodies healthy and running smoothly.

Disease, illness, or injury can cause the body to malfunction. Doctors spend many years learning about the human body and how to treat it when it does not work properly.

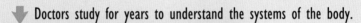

Doctors study for years to understand the systems of the body.

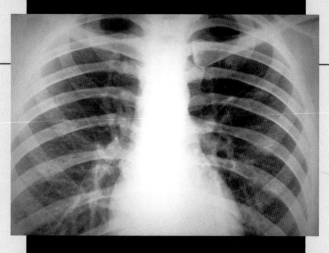

Some doctors focus on just one system of the body and become specialists in that field.

Looking at the various systems will help explain how they work and what they do. Then we can begin to better understand the body as a whole.

Imaging Techniques

Doctors often use medical imaging machines to look inside the body without performing surgery. X-rays, ultrasound, computed tomography, and MRI are some of the methods used to see inside the human body. They provide valuable information to help doctors treat their patients' injuries and illnesses.

The human body is capable of amazing things.

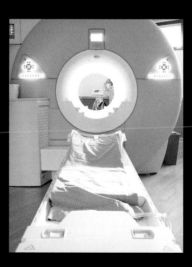

9

Cardiovascular System

The cardiovascular system reaches every part of the human body. It moves blood throughout the body and keeps the heart beating. The body cannot survive without a working heart, so this system is very important. The heart never rests. It has to constantly deliver blood and oxygen to all the organs and extremities of the body through an intricate system of arteries, veins, and other vessels designed to carry blood.

When arteries become blocked or narrow, a person can have heart problems—a condition known as coronary artery disease. CAD can cause chest pain, which may be the beginning of a heart attack. Things that may cause CAD include high cholesterol, smoking, and tension, as well as lack of exercise, a poor diet, and obesity. CAD is one of the leading causes of death in the United States.

A Beating Heart

Have you ever listened to your heartbeat? You can hear your heart through an instrument called a stethoscope. But you can feel your heart beating without using a stethoscope.

After heavy exercise, you will probably feel a pounding sensation in your chest—your heart is working hard to pump enough oxygen to your muscles and organs. The human heart works tirelessly, beating more than 2.5 billion times during an average lifespan.

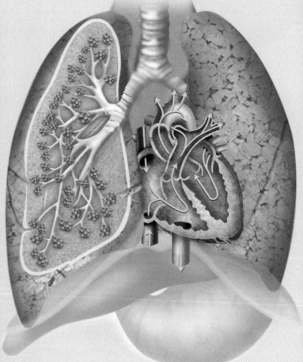

The heart is the most important part of the cardiovascular system.

One of the most important jobs of the respiratory system is to provide oxygen to the body. It also removes carbon dioxide, a waste gas produced by the body. When a person breathes air into the lungs, oxygen moves into the blood that is passing through the lungs. Then the circulatory system takes over to finish the work. Once the blood has a fresh supply of oxygen, it is transported to all parts of the body.

When the blood leaves the lungs, it leaves carbon dioxide behind. When a person exhales, or breathes out,

Did You Know?

The average human inhales and exhales about 20 times a minute. Around one-fifth of a cubic foot (6 liters) of oxygen is inhaled during each minute.

carbon dioxide is pushed out of the lungs and sent back out into the air.

The respiratory system includes several parts. The nose, mouth, and throat (pharynx) draw in air. Then air travels through the trachea, a tube that leads to the lungs. The trachea branches out into smaller tubes called bronchi and bronchioles. These airways eventually lead to thousands of tiny sacs in the lungs called alveoli.

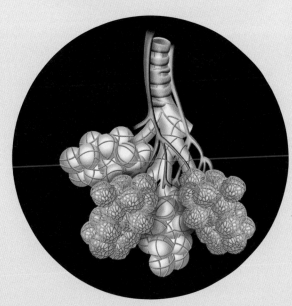

◀ Oxygen and carbon dioxide are exchanged in the lungs' alveoli.

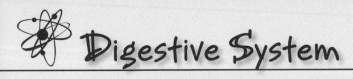

Have you ever wondered what happens to the food you eat? You probably already know that it becomes fuel for your body. But how does the body break it down and transport it to the parts that need it?

The digestive tract is part of the digestive system. The tract is made up of the mouth, esophagus, stomach, small intestine, large intestine—which includes the cecum, colon, and rectum—and the anus. There is also a layer of smooth muscle, which helps the body break down food and move it along the tract.

Additional organs such as the pancreas and liver assist the body in digestion.

The digestive process starts in the mouth, where the tongue pushes food around the mouth so the teeth can grind it up. Saliva, a digestive juice, starts the chemical process of breaking down or digesting the food so it can be absorbed by the body.

Did You Know?

The average human's stomach capacity is around 1 quart (1 liter), but the stomach can be stretched to hold up to four times that amount.

In Your System

Over the average lifetime, a person will eat around 35 tons (31.5 metric tons) of food. And it will all pass through the digestive system!

The type of food and the health of the person can affect the time it takes to digest food. Liquids such as juice and water are the easiest foods to digest, while proteins such as beans, eggs, and meat take the longest. A person's activity level and the

amount of water in his or her system also affect digestion. On average, the entire process takes about a day.

The body begins the digestive process before food even enters the mouth. Have you ever salivated while thinking about a specific food? The saliva releases enzymes, chemicals that will help the body digest the food once it has been eaten.

The esophagus pushes food down into the stomach. There digestive juices made by the pancreas (used to break down protein, carbohydrates, and fat) and the liver (used to dissolve fat) break the food down even more. A thick layer of mucus protects the stomach lining from the juices.

From the stomach, food travels about 20 feet (6 meters) through the small intestine, which transfers water and nutrients into the blood. Sugar is also digested at this point.

The body's nutrients go through the liver. The liver processes the nutrients and decides where they will be sent in the body. It also filters out harmful substances, some of which are made into digestive juices.

Finally, whatever cannot be digested moves through about 5 feet (1.5 m) of large intestine. When the body has taken out as many nutrients as it can from the waste, it gets rid of the rest.

Digestive System

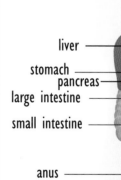

mouth
esophagus
liver
stomach
pancreas
large intestine
small intestine
anus
bloodstream

Did You Know?

The organs that digest food and eliminate wastes are sometimes called the gastrointestinal tract. Cells that line the GI tract work constantly, but they only live a few days. The body is continually replacing them with new cells that go to work immediately to digest food.

Urinary System

The urinary system works alongside the digestive system to get rid of body waste. But their functions are very different.

The digestive system eliminates the remains of food that cannot be used. The urinary system eliminates chemicals and excess fluids that are byproducts of the body's functioning. Kidneys filter the blood to remove the unwanted byproducts and keep the right amount of salts and other minerals. Then they get rid of the byproducts in urine, which is about 95 percent water.

Urine travels through the ureters and into the bladder, a sac made especially to collect and store the unwanted fluid. Several times a day, urine is released from the body through the urethra.

In a 24-hour cycle, the kidneys filter and clean about 50 gallons (190 liters) of blood and make about 3 pints (1.5 liters) of urine.

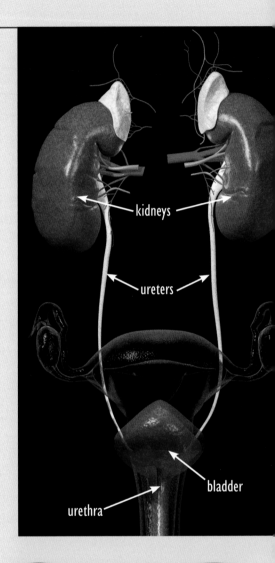

kidneys

ureters

bladder

urethra

Did You Know?

Water makes up 55 to 70 percent of the human body. Six to eight glasses of water a day help the body perform at its best. Both losing too much water and drinking too much water can be fatal.

The endocrine system releases hormones into the body that control growth, puberty, development, and even mood.

Many hormones are released by the hypothalamus, a part of the brain. The hormones travel through the blood to regulate physical changes in the body. Some hormones are released at certain times for special purposes. Growth hormones are active during childhood but slow down during the teen years. At puberty, the body makes more testosterone in boys and more estrogen in girls.

Some hormones are released as a reaction to something. The hormone adrenaline is released in times of fear or stress.

Diabetes

Diabetes is a disease that causes the body to not make or properly use insulin, a hormone made by the pancreas. It controls the amount of glucose, or sugar, in the blood.

When blood glucose levels rise, the body reacts. It makes the person very thirsty, forcing him or her to urinate more often. This is the body's attempt at flushing out the excess glucose. Over time, diabetes can cause long-term damage to the human body.

The earliest mention of diabetes was around 1550 B.C. in Egypt. The first chemical tests for diabetes were developed in the early 1800s. It was

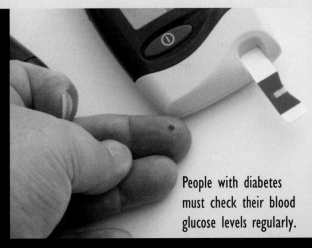

People with diabetes must check their blood glucose levels regularly.

found a way to treat the disease. They learned that insulin injected into the body by a syringe could help control sugar levels in the blood.

There are nearly 24 million people in the United States and more than 180 million people worldwide who suffer from diabetes. Every year nearly 3 million people die from the disease.

Immune System

People come in contact with germs and viruses every day. Most of the time, people don't get sick from them. They are able to fight off disease with the body's natural defense—the immune system. Our bodies are constantly battling danger, usually without even thinking about it. There are several kinds of immunity: innate, adaptive, and passive.

Innate immunity is something every human has. It includes physical barriers

HIV and AIDS

Human immunodeficiency virus damages cells that help the immune system work, making the body more vulnerable to infection. Once the cells are damaged, the condition is called Acquired Immune Deficiency Syndrome, or AIDS.

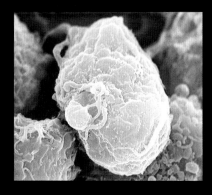

HIV can be found in body fluids such as blood, semen, vaginal fluid, and breast milk. It can be passed between people through sexual contact, sharing needles or getting a blood transfusion from someone who has HIV, or during pregnancy (between mother and baby).

HIV cannot be passed through casual contact, such as shaking hands or hugging, using public facilities such as a telephone or restroom, giving blood, or getting a mosquito bite. It also cannot be passed through tears,

More than 33 million people worldwide suffer from HIV or AIDS. As with any other disease, prevention is the best defense. However, it can be managed through drug therapies and good health care.

In November 2008, doctors in Germany claimed to have healed a patient with AIDS using stem cell therapy and a bone marrow transplant. Other scientists are using this knowledge with the

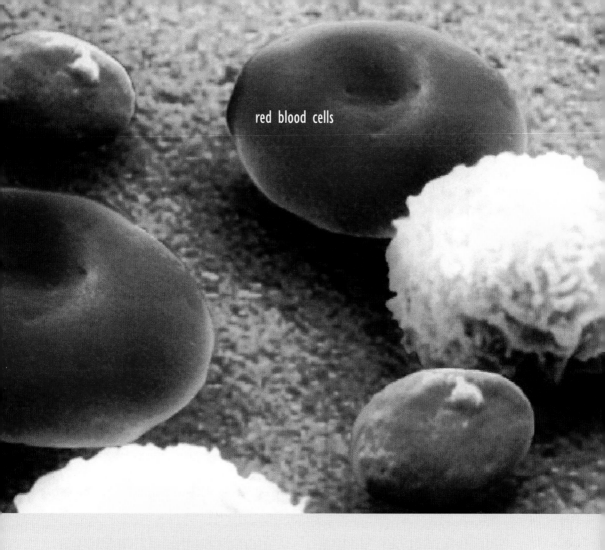

red blood cells

such as skin, as well as special chemicals in the blood and cells in the immune system. Innate immunity prevents diseases from entering our bodies, and protects us from viruses carried by other animals (such as leukemia in cats.)

Adaptive immunity develops over time as humans are exposed to or immunized against various germs and diseases. It "remembers" certain types of infections so the body can fight them off in the future.

Passive immunity is a kind of immunity borrowed from another source—for example, babies receive antibodies from their mothers' breast milk, which help them fight illnesses in the early stages of life.

Reproductive System

The reproductive system produces male or female sex cells.

The male system includes the testes, seminal vesicles, prostate gland, and penis. Sperm cells are produced in the testes. Once mature, they move into the epididymis and the vas deferens. The seminal vesicles nourish the sperm. After the prostate gland adds another fluid that allows the sperm to swim, the mixture, called semen, is ready to be released through the penis.

The female system consists of the ovaries, fallopian tubes, and uterus. Eggs are stored in the ovaries, which release one egg a month after a woman reaches puberty. The egg travels down the fallopian tube toward the uterus, where it waits to be fertilized. If it is not fertilized within 24 hours, it dies, and the cycle begins again the following month.

If semen enters the female body through the vagina, it can travel to the uterus. There a sperm cell may reach the egg and fertilize it. It then takes about nine months for the body to develop a baby.

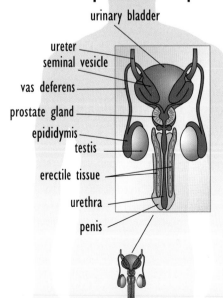

Male Reproductive System

- urinary bladder
- ureter
- seminal vesicle
- vas deferens
- prostate gland
- epididymis
- testis
- erectile tissue
- urethra
- penis

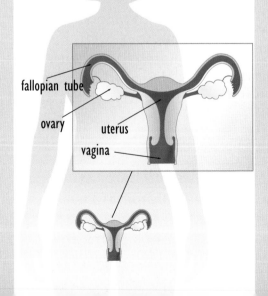

Female Reproductive System

- fallopian tube
- ovary
- uterus
- vagina

The lymphatic system consists of the lymph nodes, spleen, and tonsils. Lymph nodes, found throughout the body, contain white blood cells and fibers that destroy pathogens, such as germs and cancer cells. The spleen, located in the abdomen, filters foreign substances from the blood. Tonsils, found in the throat, prevent infections from growing in our breathing passages. During childhood, the thymus gland helps develop a strong immune system.

Did You Know?

People usually create around 100 billion white blood cells a day. White blood cells have a lifespan of only a couple of days. When the cells die, they are destroyed and replaced by living white blood cells.

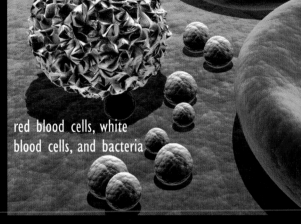

red blood cells, white blood cells, and bacteria

More About White Blood Cells

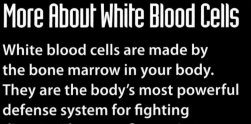

White blood cells are made by the bone marrow in your body. They are the body's most powerful defense system for fighting disease. There are five main types of white blood cells, each serving a different purpose:

neutrophils—the most common type; these cells are usually found near sites of infection

lymphocytes—produce antibodies that kill toxins created by bacteria and germs

monocytes—the largest type; they remove foreign particles and attack germs that cannot be dealt with by neutrophil cells

eosinophils—fight parasites and infection; they control reactions related to allergies and asthma

basophils—the least common type; they are often found in parasitic tissues, as well as at sites of allergic and inflammatory reactions

Integumentary System

Skin, hair, and nails make up the integumentary system. They protect the body from the outside world.

Skin

The skin is the body's largest organ—it makes up 15 to 20 percent of your total body weight. It is the body's first line of defense. It keeps germs and excess water out and the body's natural salts and fluids in. And it protects the muscles, bones, and organs from damage.

Skin is very sensitive. It can detect touch, feel pain, and distinguish between hot and cold. The skin also helps control the temperature of the body.

Skin has three layers. The epidermis, the outer layer, protects the body from water and infection. The dermis, the layer under the epidermis, provides an inner cushion against bumps and blows. It also supports hair follicles and sweat glands. The hypodermis is the lowest layer, used mainly to store fat.

epidermis

dermis

hypodermis

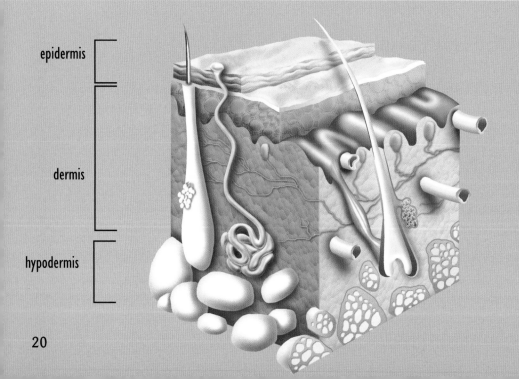

Hair

Almost every part of your body is covered with hair. Hair helps control body temperature and protects the head from harmful sunlight. Each person's hair is affected by heredity— by the genes that determine its texture, color, and growth.

Nails

The tips of the fingers and toes are very sensitive. Nails are made of hard plates of a protein called keratin. They protect and support the fingers and toes. The health of a nail can be a sign of the general health of a person.

Did You Know?

Although it's a popular belief, hair and nails do not continue to grow after death. Decomposition causes flesh to shrink, which makes the hair and nails appear longer.

All About Hair

Both human hair and nails are made of keratin. It's the same protein that makes up horns, hooves, shells, claws, and feathers in animals.

The average adult body has more than 5 million hairs. About 100,000 of these hairs grow on a person's scalp. A person loses 80 to 100 hairs each day, but they are soon replaced by new growth. A single hair can grow for several years, and then hit a resting period. Eventually old hair is pushed out of its follicles by new hair coming in.

Scientists can distinguish between six kinds of human hair—head, body, eyebrow and eyelash, beard and mustache, pubic, and axillary (armpit). They can tell whether the hair came from a person of European, Asian, or African descent, and can even find if it came from a man or a woman.

Skeletal System

The skeletal system is the framework for the entire body. It gives the body shape and supports the muscles, organs, and tissues. Where two or more bones meet, there is a joint held together by connective tissues called ligaments. Joints such as elbows and knees allow the body to move.

Certain bones sometimes protect certain organs. The rib cage protects the heart. The skull protects the brain.

The skeletal system also produces red and white blood cells and platelets for the circulatory system. Minerals are stored in the bones, ready to be used when needed.

Getting the Shivers

The human body needs to maintain a core temperature of 98.6 degrees Fahrenheit (36.6 degrees Celsius). When we get cold, we shiver.

Shivering is an automatic and subconscious response created by the body. It is caused when our skeletal muscles shake in an attempt to create warmth from energy. Shivering requires a large amount of energy and is the body's last line of defense against the cold. Automatic responses also control breathing rates, heart rates, blood pressure, and weight regulation.

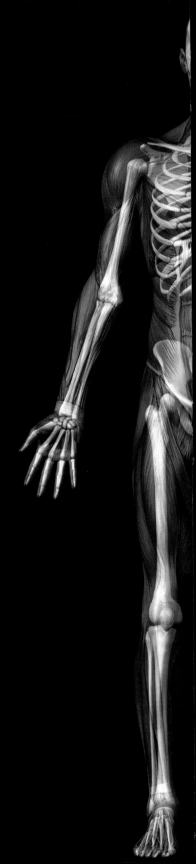

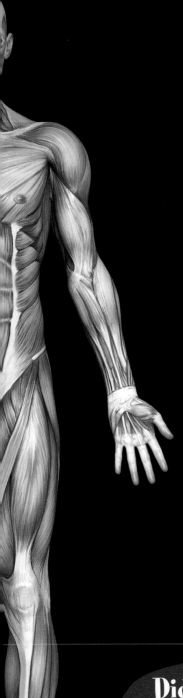

Muscular System

The skeleton could not work without the muscular system. Muscles perform all body movements. Most muscles come in pairs. One muscle pulls part of your body one way, and the other makes it go the opposite direction. This allows you to move your body parts back and forth.

There are three types of muscle: skeletal, cardiac, and smooth. Skeletal muscles attach to the bones, making the skeleton move in the direction you want it to go. Skeletal muscles are voluntary, which means you can control them when you want to run, lift, swim, or do other physical activities.

Cardiac muscles are found only in the heart. They contract constantly, making sure that the heart pumps enough blood and makes heartbeats. Cardiac muscles are involuntary, which means they work on their own.

Smooth muscles are found in the walls of blood vessels and in some organs, as well as in the throat. Smooth muscles are involuntary, squeezing when necessary to pump blood through vessels or help you swallow your food.

Did You Know?

The human body has more than 650 muscles, which make up half a person's total body weight. The muscles are attached to the skeleton by connective tissues called tendons, which allow bones to pull on muscles.

There are two parts to the nervous system—the central nervous system and the peripheral nervous system. Both parts work together to gather information and to help the body function.

The Central Nervous System

The central nervous system consists of the brain and the spinal cord. They work together to gather information from neurons, specialized cells throughout the body that send electrical impulses.

The brain is the most complex of all body parts. It makes up only 2 percent of the body, but it controls everything the body does, including involuntary activities, such as heartbeats, breathing, and digestion. The brain is also responsible for voluntary activities, such as walking and running. It even handles thinking and reasoning.

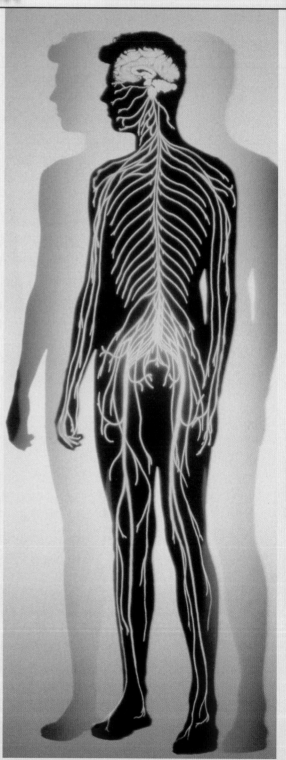

The Peripheral Nervous System

The peripheral nervous system includes the autonomic nervous system, which regulates the body's organs, and the somatic nervous system, which connects the body's limbs and organs to the central nervous system.

These systems process and react to the information received by the body. Reactions can range from simple reflexes such as blinking or stretching to physical responses such as relaxation or fear.

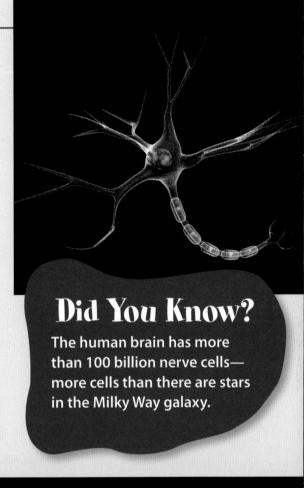

Did You Know?

The human brain has more than 100 billion nerve cells—more cells than there are stars in the Milky Way galaxy.

Instinct, Abstraction, and Emotion

Most animals depend on instincts for survival. Humans are no different. Hunger, fear, and even love come from instincts, which tell us important things about what we need to do to solve problems or get what we want.

Humans can also use abstraction, which means we can think about problems and see the big picture. We can also examine problems after they happen. Humans are able to stop and think rather than rely merely on their instincts.

An emotion is an instant response to something. It is based on feelings rather than thought. Many circumstances can cause strong emotions, such as fear or joy. An event, a thought, or even a television show can cause us to react.

Putting Science to Good Use

It's smart to start good habits early on. If you begin to take care of your body when you are young, you can avoid many health problems later. Good habits include eating healthful food, exercising, and having regular checkups with your doctor.

Adults can help kids reach their fitness goals. Support from friends and family is important. Parents can help teach good eating habits by buying and serving healthful foods. Friends can get together to exercise. A walk around the block or kicking a soccer ball is always more fun with friends.

However, many activities can also be done alone. Dance to your favorite music or put on an exercise video. Do yoga, aerobics, or martial arts in your bedroom. Try walking up and down stairs instead of taking an elevator. Some household chores can also give you a real workout.

An important part of keeping the body healthy and strong is staying active. Playing sports provides exercise and teaches people to work as a team.

Youth sports should be fun and safe. You can stay safe and healthy if you remember to follow these 10 tips:

1. Play in a safe area.

2. Play under the direction of a trained coach.

3. Play within your limits. Don't try to learn it all in a day.

4. Always wear the right equipment, especially good shoes and well-fitting safety gear.

5. Stretch and warm up before playing.

6. Know the rules of the game.

↑ Safety equipment, such as a batter's helmet, keeps sports safe.

7. Respect your teammates.

8. Respect the other team.

9. Don't play when you are injured.

10. Cool down slowly after a good workout, and be sure to drink enough throughout the day.

Sometimes healthy bodies need a doctor's care. Doctors normally provide care when people are sick, but they also offer preventive medicine to help people avoid diseases. With regular checkups, we can help our doctors help us.

Some doctors practice general medicine, and others treat specific body systems or illnesses. There are specialists called pediatricians who treat children, and geriatric physicians who treat the elderly. Some doctors are experts with the ears, nose, and throat. Cardiologists work exclusively with the heart, and endocrinologists treat patients with diabetes.

It is easy to take good health for granted. Getting proper care from medical experts and making good decisions can help our bodies stay strong and healthy.

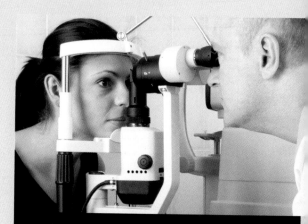

On the Job

If you like helping people, you might consider a career in medicine. You could study to become a doctor, a nurse, or another type of health care professional. If you want to pursue a career in medicine, be sure to keep your grades up, study hard, and take a lot of science courses. There are many jobs in the medical field to choose from, depending on what your interests are, including:

- physician
- nurse
- psychologist
- dentist
- dental assistant
- administrator
- medical assistant
- radiology technician
- research assistant
- massage therapist
- physical therapist
- medical technologist

Living a Better Life

It's easy to start living a healthier life. Think about your lifestyle. Change habits that hold you back from being fit. Keep the habits that lead to good health and plenty of activity.

1. What should I eat? A balanced diet is the key to good health. You can't eat too many vegetables. And be sure to limit your fats and sugars.

2. Drink lots of water. Avoid sodas and drinks that are high in sugar.

3. Keep moving! Limit your time on the computer or watching television. Instead of sitting for hours, set a timer and get up when it goes off. Then do something that uses the bones, muscles, and organs in your body.

4. Schedule physical activities. Sign up for a swim team or exercise class. Staying on a schedule means it's harder to skip sessions. You can also make friends in class and be healthy together.

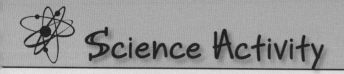

The Nose Knows

In this activity, you will test several people to see whether their abilities to smell are equal. Be sure there are no distractions. Ask yourself whether the sense of smell is more developed in some people. Or are people who seem to have good noses just more focused?

Materials

- six or more volunteers (more volunteers will give your experiment better results)

- blindfolds for the volunteers

- three or four fragrant items, such as spray perfume, scented soap, hot popcorn, flowers, warm brownies, garlic, or an orange

- stopwatch or timer

- paper

- pen or pencil

Procedure

1 Find a quiet room in which to conduct your science activity. Turn off radios, televisions, and anything else that makes noise. Close the windows. Turn off anything that affects the airflow in the room, such as air conditioners and fans.

2 Blindfold two of your volunteers and lead them into the room. Place them about 10 feet (3 meters) from the doorway. Let them sit in a comfortable position. Tell them to keep quiet and relax.

3 Tell the two volunteers to quietly raise their hands whenever they smell a new item. Tell them to think about what the smell may be.

4 Have your paper and pen or pencil ready. If possible have an assistant record the results.

opcorn Perfume Fries

37 sec 45 sec
62 sec

5 Bring the first item, a bottle of spray perfume, into the room and place it just inside the doorway. Spray some perfume into the air.

6 Record the number of seconds that passed before each volunteer raised his or her hand to indicate he or she noticed a new smell. Wait until both volunteers have raised their hands. Then ask them to identify the smell. Record their answers.

7 Repeat steps 5 and 6, using different items. Try to "trick" them from time to time, perhaps by bringing in a smell you already introduced. This will help you know whether your volunteers are accurately reporting what they smell.

8 Repeat steps 2 through 7 with other volunteers. Record the results.

9 Analyze the results. Did all the volunteers have the same sense of smell? Did some volunteers have a better sense of smell? Do you think their ability to smell correctly had anything to do with how focused they were on the activity?

Glossary

artery—blood vessel that carries blood away from the heart and to the cells, tissues, and organs of the body

cardiovascular system—system that keeps blood moving through the body

cholesterol—substance normally absorbed by the liver; buildup in blood vessels can lead to coronary artery disease

digestion—breaking down of food into simpler chemical parts

digestive system—organs in the body that digest food

endocrine system—system that consists of organs called glands that send hormones directly into the bloodstream

hormones—substances that are made in one organ and sent to others

immune system—various cells and tissues in the body that protect it from infection and disease

integumentary system—system consisting of the skin, hair, and nails

lymphatic system—interconnected system of lymph nodes that fight disease in the body

lymphocyte—white blood cell that boosts the immune system

marrow—soft tissue inside bones that produces platelets and red and white blood cells

muscular system—system composed of skeletal, smooth, and cardiac muscles; performs all body movements

nervous system—system of cells, tissues, and organs that regulates the body's responses to events and conditions

neuron—nerve cell

pathogen—microorganism, such as a virus or fungus, that causes disease

reproductive system—system that produces male and female sex cells

respiratory system—system that provides oxygen to the body

skeletal system—bones and cartilage that give structure to the body and protect internal organs

ultrasound—high-frequency sound waves used to create an image of part of the body

urinary system—system that gets rid of waste through the kidneys and bladder

vein—vessel that carries blood to the heart

virus—microscopic microorganism that can cause disease

Important People in Medicine

Caspar Bartholin (1585–1629)
Danish professor of medicine whose book on human anatomy was the standard textbook for many years

Claude Bernard (1813–1878)
The French "father of physiology," who suggested that the functions of the organs in the body are closely interrelated and that the body maintains a constant internal environment despite external changes

Elizabeth Blackwell (1821–1910)
American doctor who received her medical degree from Geneva Medical College in New York in 1849 and became the first female physician in the United States

Michael Stuart Brown (1941–   )
American geneticist who, with Joseph L. Goldstein, discovered how cholesterol is metabolized in the body; shared the Nobel Prize with Goldstein in 1985

Harvey William Cushing (1869–1939)
First American to specialize in neurological surgery; his important contributions included work on brain tumors

Paul Ehrlich (1854–1915)
German physician who was the first to use chemotherapy; shared the 1908 Nobel Prize with Ilja Mecnikov for their studies of immunity

Sir Alexander Fleming (1881–1955)
Scottish bacteriologist who discovered how the human body defends itself against bacterial infection; shared the Nobel Prize in 1945 with Sir Howard Florey and Ernst Chain for the discovery of penicillin

Galen (c. 130–c. 200)
Turkish physician who became one of the most famous and influential doctors of Rome; developed a model of the human body that for centuries was the standard for anatomy

William Harvey (1578–1657)
British physician who studied physiology, anatomy, embryology, and medicine, advancing each field; his work included the study of nutrition to improve health

Hippocrates (c. 460 B.C.–c. 370 B.C.)
Greek physician who developed ideas that led to the Hippocratic oath; he is called the father of medicine; started a school of medicine on the Greek island of Cos, where he encouraged the separation of medicine and religion

George Nicholas Papanicolaou (1883–1962)
Greek-born American physician who developed a test to diagnose diseases such as cervical cancer and sexually transmitted diseases in women; the test is commonly called the Pap smear

James Parkinson (1755–1824)
British physician and paleontologist who made the first clinical description of the condition now known as Parkinson's disease

Louis Pasteur (1822–1895)
French chemist and microbiologist who developed the germ theory of disease; developed the first vaccine against anthrax and rabies

Albert Bruce Sabin (1906–1993)
Polish-born American microbiologist and physician who invented the first oral polio vaccine, called the Sabin vaccine

Jonas Edward Salk (1914–1995)
American microbiologist and physician who formulated a polio vaccine and searched for a cure for AIDS

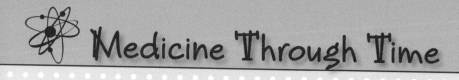
535 B.C. Human cadaver is dissected for scientific study by Greek physician Alcmaeon of Croton (Italy)

400 B.C. Hippocrates founds the profession of medicine, separates medicine from religion, and develops the Hippocratic oath

300 B.C. First anatomy book written by Diocles, a student of Aristotle

180 A.D. Galen accumulates all known medical knowledge of the time in a treatise; it was used until the end of the Middle Ages

1000 *Canon of Medicine* written by Avicenna; it was a five-volume compilation of Greek and Arabic medicine used until the 17th century

1414 First case of influenza reported in France

1500 First recorded Caesarean section to deliver a baby

1624 English physician Thomas Sydenham identifies scarlet fever and measles and uses iron to relieve anemia

1752 French scientist René Antoine Ferchault de Réaumur discovers the role of gastric juices

1832 British physician Thomas Hodgkin describes Hodgkin's disease, a cancer of the lymph nodes

1849 Elizabeth Blackwell is the first woman to receive a medical degree

1877 Louis Pasteur notes that some bacteria die when combined with certain other bacteria, which led to the first antibiotics in 1939

1879 Pasteur's discoveries lead to the development of vaccines against many diseases, including smallpox; he later creates vaccines for anthrax and rabies

1893	First open heart surgery is performed by an African-American cardiologist, Dr. Daniel Hale Williams
1896	First diagnostic X-ray taken in the United States by Serbian-American physicist and inventor Michael I. Pupin
1910	First types of chemotherapy used by Dr. Paul Ehrlich to cure syphilis
1921	Dr. Frederick Banting and medical student Charles Best discover insulin, which is important in the treatment of diabetes
1952	Jonas Salk develops the first polio vaccine
1954	American biochemist Vincent Du Vigneaud synthesizes the hormone oxytocin; he wins the Nobel Prize in chemistry the next year
1955	The Salk vaccine for polio comes into use
1960	Cardiopulmonary resuscitation (CPR) is invented
1967	First successful heart transplant is performed in South Africa by surgeon Christiaan Barnard
1981	AIDS is recognized for the first time; vaccine for hepatitis B is developed
1982	Human insulin is genetically engineered from a type of bacteria
2003	Carlo Urbani, doctor for the World Health Organization, identifies the first outbreak of SARS, triggering the most effective response to an epidemic in history; Urbani dies from the contagious respiratory disease a month later
2009	Shipment of tainted peanut products infects nearly 600 people with salmonella; more than 125 different foods are recalled

Cassan, A. *Introduction to the Human Body*. Philadelphia: Chelsea House, 2006.

Cooper, Sharon Katz. *Human Body Systems: Maintaining the Body's Functions*. Minneapolis: Compass Point Books, 2007.

Cooper, Sharon Katz. *Major Organs: Sustaining Life*. Minneapolis: Compass Point Books, 2007.

Gold, Martha V. *The Nervous System*. Berkeley Heights, N.J.: Enslow, 2004.

Gray, Susan H. *The Heart*. Chanhassen, Minn.: Child's World, 2006.

Newquist, H. P. *The Great Brain Book: An Inside Look at the Inside of Your Head*. New York: Scholastic Reference, 2004.

Internet Sites

FactHound offers a safe, fun way to find Internet sites related to this book. All of the sites on FactHound have been researched by our staff.

Here's all you do:

Visit *www.facthound.com*

FactHound will fetch the best sites for you!

Index

Connie Jankowski

Connie Jankowski is a seasoned journalist, marketing expert, public relations consultant, and teacher. Her education includes a bachelor of arts degree from the University of Pittsburgh and graduate study at Pitt. She has worked in publishing, public relations, and marketing for the past 25 years. Jankowski is the author of 11 books and hundreds of magazine articles.

Image Credits